OLIVER BERNARD · VERSE &C.

Also by Oliver Bernard

POETRY

Country Matters
Poems 1983

TRANSLATIONS

Apollinaire: Selected Poems
Rimbaud: Collected Poems

MEMOIRS

Getting Over It

Oliver Bernard
Verse &c.

ANVIL PRESS POETRY

Published in 2001
by Anvil Press Poetry Ltd
Neptune House 70 Royal Hill London SE10 8RF

Copyright © Oliver Bernard 2001

ISBN 0 85646 332 9

This book is published
with financial assistance from
The Arts Council of England

A catalogue record for this book
is available from the British Library

Designed and set in Monotype Bulmer by Anvil
Printed and bound in England
by Cromwell Press, Trowbridge, Wiltshire

IN MEMORY OF BRUCE BERNARD

ACKNOWLEDGEMENTS

Moons and Tides, Walberswick was first printed and published in 1978 by Paul Nicholson, under the imprint Mirror Press, Bangor, North Wales.

Five Peace Poems was published in 1985 by Five Seasons Press. Three of these poems appeared in *For Life on Earth* (ed. Maggie Gee); in the first issue of *Rialto*; and in *Encounter*.

The Finger Points at the Moon was first published by Tuba Press in 1989 to coincide with the bicentenary of the French Revolution and the retirement from the French House in Dean Street, Soho – formerly the York Minster – of Gaston Berlemont.

Quia Amore Langueo was published as the first translation of the complete Middle English poem by Blackfriars Publications in 1991.

None of the remaining poems in this volume has ever appeared in book form, though many were first printed in magazines such as *Ambit*, *Encounter*, the *New Statesman*, the *Spectator*, *New Poetry* etc. Two of them contributed to a festschrift for George Barker in 1973.

Contents

XLVII Poems

I

Starting from what is possible we arrive
At places we would hardly have dared to aim for:
But no one sets out from the frozen pole
Or reaches it by sailing.
I have not brought you back a traveller's tale.

All of us are survivors,
And it is not important why we are spared
So long as we are aware that we have been
Passed over.
Passed over by dangerous childhood
Frightening adolescence,
The age of reason,
Military age,
The age of consent.
Survivors of war and of a peace where anything
Can happen and often does:
Death on the highway, pox on the street corner;
Dry rot hurling masonry on to tunnelled pavements;
"Acts of God", disasters of all descriptions, floods,
Experimental explosions, and the winter:
Domestic accidents, falls in the darkened stackyard,
Electrocution, fire and suicide.

There are always a few
Who refuse the passive voice;
Others will argue.
But there is no arguing with the facts:
The usual tests
Will reveal a pulse however faint,
A respiration however stealthy.

We cloud the mirror,
And waving a flag our blood is always ready
To break out of this dark corporeal castle.

II 5 Poems for Photographs

for Elizabeth Graham

1 *(Leaf shadows on tree trunk)*

In in the wood the path
closes behind you. Trees
consult and blend as shadow.
In in the darkness lie
the weight of photosynthesis,
the decadence of leaves,
the wet of unseen sky.
If canopy is pierced
by splash or chink of sun
the shadow play of leaf
(a hand flicked across bark)
is quicker than the eye.
you hardly see the trees
and cannot find the wood.

2 *(Fishing pier, frozen mere)*

Under the March sky
and the sign of Pisces,
below the ranked woods
and the silver surface,
beneath all possibility
of human breath,
the humble rejoice:

No one is fishing,
we are being spared,
the water authorities

maintain the level
of our element,
even the anglers
grow obtuse
at their firesides;
and He,
He will not break
the bruised reed.

3 *(Sawn beech stump, dry grasses)*

The motes among the beams
In grey green spaces of air
Held within boughs like arms
Uplifted from the bare
Beautiful trunk. And lace
Of early leaves floating
Like fair weather clouds
Or layers of smoke in still
and sunlit places.

Dead. Felled. Cut up
And carted away.
The stump sawn clear,
Level with the forgetting soil
And the invading growth
Of everything that's less
And takes its opportunity.

Look at this upturned eye's
Iron frilled annular stare.
Nerve ends. No heroic
History. Just years.
Years. Some dry, some good.
Memorial of itself.
The fact is, wood.
Truth is the living tree.

4 *(Frozen tussocks, wire fence, winter light)*

summer knows
better than I do
what she's up to
as she goes

taking long
strides among
Australian plains
Andean passes

behind her back
these short days
frost stiffens
the tired grasses

these short days
these long nights
love grows and grows
summer knows

5 *(Iron field gate in the snow)*

Rest-harrow, charlock, were
Their ordinary weeds,
Whose gates and ploughs were made
Of iron, oak,ash; who laid
Head to warm flank to milk
And heard it spurt like silk,
Who smelt the cow's sweet breath
Blood-warm in winter's death

And now no more are found
Than grasshopper on ground
Or cockchafer in air
Though summer's everywhere.

I'll be a-goin', they'd say.
I' hed enough o' this ol' day.

III   evening

for R.

begins your hour gold above blue
horizon and green among pearls
the weeds lash gently in the flood
tide the moon climbs now unfurls
the long banner the new device

a scaring dazzle all white day
the sky relents with colours and
evening comes into the room
through the big window takes your hand
farewell but then forgets to go

sending you I here observe
something like a poem though
a friend's poems how difficult
it was your hour the moon is so
(pale and three-quarters) like your face

IV   You

You, if I say that brilliant
Upsetting vocable this verse
Staggers before it's learnt to crawl
And howls until you take it up:
No pride not even consciousness
Of being; only wanting your
Having it to you and can sleep
Then and then only: can no more
Than sleep but if after a time
Of sleep it stirs it murmurs rhyme.

V

rockveined thunder a revealed
river on the map of cloud
instantly (so retina
burns to remember) hidden
                         loud
nothing for a space of time

nothing for the length and depth
of glassy air under the grey
bulge of drum
               then the long word
leaning farther out I say
further to incite it Thunder

drops
       then here and hissing pours
the river boils like lead the bright
flashing stand back from the taps
rain closes in like walking night

afterwards puddles stare like snow

VI   Truth

for Anna Clarkson

She goes away. When she was there
She had these dark and point-blank eyes;
I felt her sweetly lethal stare,
Endured her gaze which never lies:
And that is why I sojourn here.

– Well, hang about, till they untie
My wrists and bag me up to bury
Under the nettles and the sky.
And am I sad? Well, no, not very.
I knew the price of being I.

Don't bother now to sigh or pray.
I had it good. I had it made.
I lived my life. I had my day.
(Do dogs get stood as we get laid?)
But, as for Truth, she goes away.

VII   My Imperfect Host

(Dennis Silk, October 1984)

The beetle on his door-sill
Respectable as a funeral
Was invited to go outside
As kindly as the poet
Asks you which chair
You find most comfortable
Gently and inquiring
With his whole moonish face
And most attentive eyes
About the health of one
Who is not at the party
Where he goes to the kitchen
To find the things to eat
And another bottle of wine
He fetched from the Old City
Earlier in the day

The beetle was not unwelcome
Or at all disliked
But he had I understood
Let in several others
Before this one blundered
Down on the threshold
And there is perhaps not a limit
But a moment when
One begins to be aware
Of frankly too many beetles
Visiting at a time
Even the handsome gentleman
Like Sir Moses' landau

Under the Windmill might
From this point of view
Be considered *de trop*

The poor are always with us
But who can refrain from tears
At the sensitive kindness
Of my imperfect host
Whose perfect humanity
Shines out from under
Those very innocent eyebrows
Assuring you of his
Complete attention

Whose mind is a clean room
Recently swept
Containing a bed a chair
And an open window

NOTE FOR NON-JERUSALEMITES: Sir Moses Montefiore visited
Jerusalem many times (he was a great benefactor) travelling from Haifa
in a landau across the bandit-infested intervening country.
The Windmill is a Jerusalem landmark and memorial. The landau is
preserved there.

VIII   For Paul Nicholson

Yes. We are all of us
alive alone naked
for what it is worth
and for what it is worth
it is worth being
our simple selves
our very complex selves.
What disguise
can hide us from God's eyes?
What distrust is not absurd
of dust for dust?
Love one another
and die? Yes.
Because we must.
Next time I die
if you love me
remind me:
That's life.

IX   For John Stavers

He is walking running dawdling home still;
There are still chances. I remember it too well.
This was a fine day to think about him: clear
From horizon to horizon.

The lolly stick and the sandwich bag flutter
By dandelions on concrete edges. The moon
Has run away with the end of the beanstalk
And burnt my mouth

The wall has fallen on him, the houses have fallen,
The streets of the town have caused him injuries.
The tarmac grieves. In a whirling brakedrum shrieks
His guardian angel.

People are good but they do not always understand;
They do what they can but often it is not enough.
No one can change the past, however present
And not to be borne.

The faulty erratic unreliable world
Goes blundering on, and I who am certain of nothing
Pray for John who is finished with doubting forever
      and gone
Past understanding.

X   For John Minton, 1957

your face is always sad you look
as anxious as a dog your hands
fall in your lap lie anyhow
I hope to God God understands
my praying how I hope there's none

their faces haunt me worse than yours
the ignorant and heartless boys
who self-absorbed in cruel games
could not know kindness being toys
wound and set going till they killed

rawhanded read and wrote with pain
understanding how beautiful
they were (but dumb meant nothing though
you laughed they were and others will
make that discovery again)

their innocent and open eyes
do not crowfoot or criticise
pouch with fatigue or anxiousness
they have no nerves and are not wise
blue nothing looks out on a world

without meteorology
only the climate light and dark
the boys were everywhere the same
in Barcelona and Hyde Park
dumb beautiful and dressed to kill

your face is not unkind but sad
anxious inside your head your hands
do nothing now but lie and wait
I hope to God God understands
And pray Him not to be but bless

XI   For Elizabeth Smart, 1986

Yestreen the queen was calling from
Her window in the summer dusk:
'I haven't got anything nice for you.'

I came back with some cans and drank
Across the table from you while
With my authoritative voice
And timid soul I told you yours
Were real woman's poems, not
Pretended man's or pretty girl's.

But I can't judge or understand
Such lavish generosity
As the Dell garden and the kids'
And grownups' parties were a sign of.
Herbs and firewood fill my garden;
I live small. All I possess
After you've gone's what I remember
Giving you: some oyster mushrooms
From a fallen elm tree trunk.

I can't say I feel bad. I don't
Grieve. The day is still the day.
On the bright side, even, as
I travel up to Soho from
Diss Station which we shared for a bit.

In Flood Street forty years ago
You from the burnished sofa smiled
Transatlantically remote,
Warm as the sun that warmed your hand:

And now you've gone victorious
Under aconites and oakleaves
Out of what claims to be the real
World, but where angels sometimes drink,
And all we children know that love's
To do. And still I haven't done.

XII

light through branches engenders
illusions perceptions and I stand in the wood
wet leaves heraldry the drip of diamonds
the stoat leaps like a flame at the pearlcoloured throat
of a monstrous and hysterical rabbit
dark periwinkle leaves cross rotten bark
my legs tremble a little from standing still
forgetful bird begins to sing again
making a world whose radius is earshot

XIII My Spanish Friend

for Maria

She says: "We don't call Jesus 'Lord':
We call him *Señor*, you know, Mister.
And he was never a King. The Romans
Called him that to insult him. Why
Call him King and remove him
From the ordinary people?"

She says: "We don't use the word
Worship. We go to church to pray.
Why 'worship'? They are worshipping
Themselves. We are all worshipping
Our rightness, our goodness,
Our respectability
And the fact that we
Are not like the others.

"As for the Glory of God,
It isn't in churches. That is just
The glory of money. Look:
Even the cathedral
Is the glory of Norwich, not God.
If you want to see the glory
Of God, look at the way the earth
And the sky behave this morning;
Look at the child
Running across the grass!"

XIV Cross

for Sr. Alies Thérèse of Peace

When I see you cross (it's how I see you
this afternoon) bearing with difficulty
bad weather in the body: electric storms
rain and fog and for a change chill
in the damn bones, the probably blessèd bones,

I don't know if you're cross with yourself for being
less of a champ than you want to be, or cross
with the body that won't do the spirit justice,
and cross to be locked so neatly into it.
But what I know is this: I really care.

I am reminded more today than usual:
unthinking pleasure, even happiness,
doesn't quite do it. What does it is sad,
is bad news for your friend: you're not, right now,
feeling too terrific, are you? Well,

I put a couple of miles between us, sailing
into the harbour of knowing that I care.
Can't telephone to see if you're recovering,
it's too soon; and then soon it's getting late.

Philip is ill. Perhaps he has begun
to die. Everyone says how nice he is,
how brave and good Libby his wife is; but
I want to tell them God is good and we

are going to die and might as well (or better)
stop all this overemphasis on how
nice we all are. You're not nice: magic, maybe.
(Now you see it, Alies: now you don't)

XV I Grow Old – and Somewhat Religious

Hesitating in the cramped kitchen,
More of my weight on one foot than the other,
Daylight diamonded through sweaty glass,
I see the gas bottle, the shabby squares
Of carpet, the spare bowl under the sink.
The voice of my careful head is clear and silent,
And 'what am I looking for?' is what it says.

What am I looking for? I was putting sticks
Into the stove. I see the plastic strainer,
The empty milk bottle, the frying pan,
The dusty can of Italian olive oil.
It isn't these. But there's the empty teapot.
Something. And then the winter light reminds me:
The kettles to fill. I fill them at the tap
And put them on the stove which is getting hot.

What am I looking for? The revolution?
The far off happy land? The next election?
My cup of tea is simply this kingdom of heaven,
Now: and – as in the penny catechism –
'To be happy with him for ever in the next.'

XVI

the wonder of landscape is to the wonder of people
as two plus one is to the square root of minus nothing
by which I mean that if you are very careful indeed
you can do the sum but to begin to get a grasp of the
    concept
you have to have help and I know that I am the man
who was beginning to be cured of his blindness and
    cried out
I see men as trees walking and was filled with the wonder
    of it

except that I'm not at all sure that I shall be cured
in my case there seem to be hints of a possible relapse
if I don't go on looking if I don't keep trying to see
it will all go away again and my eyes only express salt
    water

sometimes it seems to help to get it all down on paper
as if registering and recording the occasional remission
gave you something to hold on to but it is just pieces of
    paper
you are holding is it or can you read again what you have
    written
and feel again as sure as you felt when you wrote it
or can you leave these pieces of paper on the table in the
    room upstairs
with your corpse on the bed with its shoulders turned to
    the wall
and think that they will be found and not lit to see
    whether
you really are dead yes I'm sorry but this time you are

XVII   Tennyson Poem

These are the loveliest evenings: gentle leaves
Lazily sift the breezes; flowers let fall
Sweetness in air. To all that easily grieves,
These days of early summer but recall
Earlier summer days, and so enrich
The season that it seems there is good in grief
If grief can weep upon these evenings which
Turn gentle in the breeze as a green leaf.

XVIII   West Harling

Under the lime trees' yellow leaves and damp
October sunlight, out of the wind and warm,
Nature's unnaturally kind this autumn.
But four young people take me for a walk
To a deserted church in good repair,
And one says weather will be like this now:
Warm and not as it used to be, with storms
And droughts that last for months, and the landscape
    changing.
And life being rarer and perhaps confined
To unlikely regions, soon not possible.

We visit the churchyard and stare in through glass
Panes at the silence of the lectern, pews
Gathering fine dust. Possibly even bats
Don't find a toehold in this shut up place
Restored and then used once a year since then.
Norfolk's a dream of how things might have been,
A different proposition from the life
We all return to, Monday. Something narrow
About the present moment if we ever
Managed to live in it and nowhere else.

XIX

Good night you'd wonder who or why
suddenly out of nowhere said
and laughed absurdly pleased alone
to speak it on the way to bed
brushing my teeth in case I smile

Tomorrow if it comes you will
see me if we meet and look
otherwise and innocent
of me my mind this open book

how can you be in some small poem?

XX

afternoon sunshine a fine rain of hair
queen snip behind me kneels the summer air
plays round her bare waist and my ticklish shoulders

cool elbows hover angels round my head
she lily gilds me with slim whispering steel
ice cream has nothing on the smile I feel

half naked aping samson on the grass
I lay aside my jawbone of an ass
the philistines stroll unmolested by

castration complex permanently waived
having it cut off's painless in such weather
pleasant if you can get it done by heather

XXI

good Friday cars drew up and stared
across the liver coloured water
some of their drivers seemed prepared
to stay till dusk somebody's daughter
twisted the mirror tangle haired

these went who came some angels made
cups of tea and contemplated
northwest skies fresh winds obeyed
necessities and agitated
reeds and waves while children played

only the clocks were busy this
wasted afternoon the sun
dazzled the gravel where the kiss
of cloudy wavelets made all run
glistening in non human bliss

XXII

I stand in the warm and draughty flat
It is May in the windowbox and in the street
And I think I am in a peculiar state of love

My suffering may be imaginary but it is none the less real
My anxiety is about nothing but I am anxious all right
My state which has to do with some idea of love
Is not precisely the state of being in love
Because I cannot really be in love by myself let alone with

But at least I am here in this state
                              hungry but not wishing to eat
The uncertainty about everything is in my hands
They tremble and almost flutter as I do inside by body

The suffering has grown less because I am removed
                              in time and space from its cause
But the uncertainty has made me open to things and to
    people
I am tenderly even absurdly glad to see them
Although I know I cannot help them much and they
    cannot help me much

Still the awareness is heightened and I ought to thank god
    for it

XXIII   New Cross Baths in the Fifties

In the sobbing aquamarine under the lamps,
  under the skylight blistered with tears,
    black blue from the sky beyond,
      winds between and the seasons lengthened to years:

Reaching along this reach, pushing off,
  strength swallowed in watery rush,
    I begin again the stroke of a long duty.
      Water boils at my nostrils.

And coming towards it look up at,
  and going away from it think of,
      the sphinx clockface, the irretrievable time,
     the baths clock up on the tiled wall
        white in the style of Greenwich Tunnel.
      Sixty-five lengths is a mile.

My legs wonder sleepily
  what is the glistening
    inelastic resistance?
      The floor. Do Not Run.

I do not care any more under the shower.
  Heat spreads in my shoulders.
    What I have done I have done.

XXIV Father and Son

he says / I don't want to be a daddy in fact I'm going to kill myself when I'm twelve / because that is the age at which he has been told one develops pubic and underarm hair and is fertile // but when he hears how males fertilize females he smiles and laughs and says I like the way it is done

and after that he is happy for a bit / but then along come I his daddy or father as I call it / and everything is still all right / he gets the tap turned on for the hose and plays it on them his sisters and little Paul / but then I say Have you turned it on harder? And he has but says no / and I see it is not so

I think I ought never to give him the opportunity of telling lies / or put him to the necessity of doing so as it were / but no one can be protected so what can I do?

I say to him it is no good my thinking he is a baby / and it is no good him thinking I am a fool / because we are both sensible people // I say this hoping of course / and he agrees I suppose hoping

We have some ice cream really water ice which is much better than good / I say I've never bought anything so good as this in a shop / no says he and you never will

you never will / that's a good saying he says / it's a good saying for mummy and her ice cream

he is quite happy and goes out / still with a few spots on him from the chicken pox / and after five or ten minutes he comes back somewhat downcast / he says John has said he doesn't like that ice cream about which he said You never will

he cries about that / is it about that? / and I say never mind he's always saying things he doesn't mean / I think a lot of people do that because they're afraid of being laughed at / you know if you say something is nasty nobody laughs at you / but if you say you like something they can

people are silly if they're afraid of being laughed at he says / his elastic world is quite clear and logical thank you / and everything means something if you want it to

I want it to

XXV   For Joe Aged 10

of course you're right and life and death
are what we always breathe in/out
and what we've done till now's survive
I recognise you wept about
the dreadfulness of these extremes

only you don't and no one has
to live and play both ends against
his diaphragm or choose between
knives poison falls road accidents
just to befall those whom it hurts

like hell to care for quite as much
as sometimes he's aware he cares
and mostly when he or they are
to leave each other soon and there's
no time to say I love you all

the time but often only know
this at the wrong time (it's too late)
what if we never meet again
oh Joe how very sad our fate
except that you forget the times

you stand on as you say there's none
but snap the telescope up shut
and live a little in the now
consider that we in the gut
know very well we carry death

all through our lives which sometimes seem
so very long I don't know if
you ever feel this boredom well
all tiredness carries a whiff
of death and so I'm going to sleep

XXVI

Now they are all at it; the sparrows at least;
And the more light it grows the mistier it gets.
The kettle's applause, including whistles, increases;
And in the middle of these noises I am sitting
Trying to make some sense of all this light.

XXVII

I am kneeling by the fire like Yeats's old woman
and my knees feel the close dampness of the rug
the smoke is in my clothes and in my mind.
I come back to this: I am a man crouched
in front of a fire. I forget everything
the conversation in the pub the way she dresses
journeys painful and joyful, the lies people take
for approximate truth the approximate beer
the hours cut out of living and referred to as work.

The bark catches and a long yellow flame
is waving its flag. What is it to me
who wins who loses I cannot share my life
if I shared myself the other share was wasted
or perhaps not but nothing lasts
and our improvements will be put in double quotes
when time has passed over us and left us unknown
how could we be known for what we are?

I am an old woman gentle and slightly bitter
I am the one to whom it is happening
I am kneeling by the fire and the fire is whispering
all those things passed and so will these.

XXVIII   From the Spanish

Manuel Flores is going to die
That's the common coin of knowledge
Dying is an ancient custom
Well kept up by common people

Tomorrow the bullet will arrive
With forgetfulness enclosed
Merlin said and Merlin knew
Dying is but being born

All the same it hurts me
To say goodbye to life
It never switches off it's so
Sweet and so familiar

In the dawn I see my hands
In my hands I trace the veins
With surprise I look at them
As if they were not really mine

So many things these eyes have seen
Since they began their travelling
And who knows what they shall see
After Christ has judged me?

Manuel Flores is going to die

XXIX

There is only, there are only, target
And non target: 1, 3, 5, 7, 9
But nothing anywhere else. Those are the rules.
There is or are also only you
And other people thing place time or mode.

To consider target. Starting from nothing everywhere,
You have 1, white, standing for all the blank
Duck scoring snow wide unsignificant world.
3 black most erring within blank not good
Charred boundary to disaster (some survivors).
5 blue the first most cold most innocent
The colour of perhaps; perhaps least human;
Blue shock wave splinters death beyond the visible.

Red 7 in love with terribly getting warmer
Suddenly tapped reserves and nerves exposed
When thou art dead yes then of shame of anger
Of lust of love of fire of fruit of rose.

Gold 9 three threes three graces sisters apples
Pollen and lightning dancing on a pinpoint.
Gold. My omegaton. I am. The sun.

XXX

Twenty miles at 75 mph
to have a cup of coffee with you in Norwich
you have bought a new secondhand blouse and I
see beautiful shadows inside it

we walk in our living dream across
pavement and roadway and stop to embrace
now and then like drunken teenagers
at times I know and you know we should be locked up

if we went swimming I should hiss
on entering the water let the sea be cold
your blouse is a shiny skin you take my hand
your upper lip lifts the bird flies into the tree

XXXI Laxfield

Pure winter and a barking dog
Loud on the candied roadway is
The only red brown patch in dawn's
Powder blue and spider grey
Until it stops and goes away

Hard coal burns brighter for the cold
Outside dawn widens into day
Where owls were calling tractors roar
The birds are silent and just may
Not survive the frost till noon

The hollies in the hedge stand up
Young tractor drivers stare into
The yellow window as they pass
And wonder as I wonder who
Writes on his pad behind the glass

XXXII   For Albert Camus

died January 1960

I'm still alive Caligula
shrieks between stabs because he knows
to live is sin enough and triumph
over the pricks of each of those
justicers except the last

while death's respectable and war
renders all fairer than love can
you may prefer the statesmanlike
approach to living but a man
may not have time to learn to die

cars crash Renoir tied brushes to
his wrist my entrails say it's spring
there will be time to pray from stone
lips to deaf heaven but this thing
I do not ask forgiveness for

XXXIII

You have slept and are awake, your tongue has partly
   forgotten its language;
Your hair blown dark by the wind that blows the wet leaves
   reminds me of dreams;
Your mouth which is slow to smile smells of toothpaste and are
   you going to bed again?
Your eyes are clear like the morning but your look is slow like
   the first time.

What is it in you that makes the day come alive? do your eyes
   caress things?
Is everything born under the touch of your honest ignorant
   hand?
Is your creation mine? Does that account for the marvellous
   newness?
The feeling that I who love you have for the moment become
   you?

XXXIV   T. S. Eliot Visits a Corsican Café

Old Capponi walks the boards,
Struts to Brighton, hands behind
A shiny crooked back. In there
Some poker player's change of mind
Provokes a hot exchange between
Morelli and a younger man
With two pairs and a pile of chips;
But sense enough. The Corsican
Hunting dogs in ordures seek
Their quarry: on those cliffs the moon
Lays her cheek; potato peel
And onion skins, and bones. But soon
The dogs fall out and bark. An ass,
His nose in it for cabbage stalks,
Sticks out a silvered rump from where
Another heap is. Cappo' talks
Growling, a change from grinding his
Grey molars, to another old
Spectator by the fire which is
Wood burning: but the moon is cold.

XXXV

You colour glad to be betrayed
I find you where you simply are
We've dropped out of the motorcade
And off the road and left the car
And walked and run and aren't afraid

Breakfast's a picnic where we eat
And drink each other with our eyes
Tasting all smooth and sharp and sweet
And tender as the faint surprise
That parallels should somehow meet

Country of milk and heather where
Sulks the dark and pouting flower

Returning to your eyes and hair
After a minute or an hour
I find your face is also bare

XXXVI

For my sister, Lake Vyrnwy:
Because of the fairy tower
And the marathon and majestic dam.
The authorities, what between wonder and curiosity,
Welsh mountain slopes and Liverpool Corporation
    drinking water –
A hundred thousand million speakers will now
Wet their municipal whistles –
Have had to ban swimming and even parking to
    rubberneck.
I suppose you could park further on and then walk back,
    though.

A friend I used to what is called create
What are called brochures with and trade and technical
Advertisements for engineering firms
Says that there is a Transylvanian
Victoria and Albert sort of posh
Hotel at the far end of the dam with fishing
Rights and a panelled library and solid
Sun never sets type comfort. Yes. How much?

But I knew I'd been right and righter than I knew
To give Lake Vyrnwy to my sister for living
By in the style to which she has become
Accustomed now to say that she's accustomed.
May all the fairies in her fairy books
And all the princes too receive her with honour.

XXXVII   Two Poems after Eluard

1

The last song of a bird lends dark wings
To the hours of silence to the hours of sleep
The last bird's beak closes over my eye
Room without floor or walls from which I shine

I remember the enormous ocean of noon
I remember the landscape swept by the rays of the sun
Sheen of the colour of lead on a storm of gold
I thrive in summer the heat fills me with wonder

I remember that girl with yellow hair and grey eyes
Her forehead her cheeks her breasts bathed in green and
    moonlight
I remember the hard opaque street in which the pale sky
Hollowed a pathway as one hollows a kiss

I remember the uncertain movements of my dreams
In forgotten beds and how from a cloudless body
Sprang a violent body dressed in desires and chains
The heat by turns isolates me and strips me

Here only is rejoicing
In this egg which the earth and daylight have incubated
Rest in the summer night

2

Face without season;
Face, window and stone;
The walls of the house resemble me like a mask:
They are fixed to my flesh.

The sun grows round,
Young, like a woman. From the wall
Of motionless paintwork
Stones start out.

In the stones, reading from left to right,
A child is sitting next to an old man:
A face.

In the distance
My mother
Dances like a wisp of dust.

XXXVIII   Visiting Lecturer

Ego wolfs the road unloads
other people's hedges grass
patches bumps and sewerage schemes
all headlights roar and flat grey arse
towards St Osyth's College yes

Ego stumbles into art
art talk at least wants to let rip
knows everything except his part
privately groans enjoyed your trip
sits staring at his plucking hands

Sweet Muse take over scrub me bare
and hang me out to dry at last
there where I cease too much to care
where future blows a kiss at past
and ego washes off my face

XXXIX   We Happy Few

for Trevor Cox

Two I admit is few
the fewest to call we.
Happy is something else.
I give you hero me
climbing over that gate
out into the dark
of nettles and overhang
of trees. Of almost park.
There is the silence there.

You might have a great swing
on the curved bough
of that magnificent beech:
a single rope
a single boy
might swing on
out over the valley.

But I give you my
unaltered hero me
climbing into the dark.
What do I see?
whatever it is, I climb
over into the dark.

Happy I don't know

But if for you sun
warm again stone
breeze lift leaf
birds of all feathers come
morning stretch out in silence?

XL I. M. Norman Mommens

for Patience Gray

Stone killed, step by stone step.
Stone stayed where it was.
Norman died in his skull
Who had lived in his heart
Which was not a heart of stone.

Here are the stone angels,
Cherubim, seraphim, standing tall;
Norman's angels.
There are also paper angels,
Sugar angels, angels carved in wood;
But angels immaterial and vast –
You might mistake them for the Northern Lights –
Are with him now.

Human angels sing him upward,
Their feet on the ground.
Human, they brew coffee;
Human, eat the olives
Of last autumn's harvesting;
Normanno, Pazienza, Spigolizzi.

Norman lived one life
But the angels from his hand,
Their feet on the earth,
Arms stretched into the sky,
Still grow, still mature,
Becoming classical, even.
Shall I never grow old enough to see them
Before I see him?

XLI

She is with strenuous arch tracing
With a mind of care thinking
How is everything, meaning
Her and other people's children's
Comings and stayings and for god's sake
Food and shelter everything personalities
Going to be arranged for? To get through
Our life how much actual contact with
Soap and water flour fluff bedclothes
Crockery dust dough?
                Or contemplate:
The small rug with the subtly interrupted
Pattern is a product of middle eastern
Thinking but not about too much at once.

XLII

You're off to school then in the morning Joe.
This is to say I hope it's not too stupid.
You understand, it's this one mainly fears
Apart from cars and anger (they are, too).

I don't care much what others think they think
About us; or what methods or religious
Attitudes they adopt: I just don't want you
To suffer unexplained indignities.

Never be no one, even when completely
Ignored or misconstrued. Don't let discredit
Come upon our old preschool university
Where steam-engines and peacocks were main subjects,
And steaming coffee, stinging cocacola,
Adequate kicks. You have been using English
For years: not for your ears the admonitions
I waste so long escaping (they don't move).

You walk it, careful, as I used to walk
Into my truant woods. But forget me, Joe.
All you have worth remembering is pleasure;
Pleasure and danger. What do I advise you?
Be yourself if you can possibly get away with it.

XLIII

Possibly after all it's not that I can't
write about Joe for instance because he insists
So much on his existence that I never
have time to choose a word to put down next
to a word that chose itself because I wonder
what the domestic hell's the matter now.

Possibly it's not that. Late at night
after I've done the fires and read half a novel,
having brushed my teeth and lit a cigarette
in the at long last quiet house, I can see
Joe asleep under his Indian blanket.

I love him as I listen to the breath
of wind in the roof. They are all better than gold,
my wife and children asleep: they aren't a drag.
I love them without a trace of anxiety;
not one part per million, not so much as there is
hydrocyanic acid in a fernleaf.

It is this loving that is not contemplation
that seems to make making poems about them absurd.
Like tossing a book called Teach Yourself to Swim
to a drowning family. Kate can't read long words yet;
and who cares about style?

XLIV

behind Bangor Mountain
mountains with drifts and pockets
of snow mountains of Wales

at the window the wind
sunnily rattles and pushes
gulls over slate roofs hover

sycamores stretch and reach
in gestures designed for forgiving
the non-living cuboids designed for
teaching and mainly for learning

God is not idly contemplating
between ionosphere and angels
the life of this wellbehaved town
but making love of the very
ink in this fountain pen
and clenching some toes in their shoes

XLV Doubts in Orchard Street

On the way from Anglia Square
To Heigham Street over the bridge
Over the Wensum I am starting
Another train of thought, walking.

Though I love crossing myself
And think pious ejaculations
Good if they come naturally
I'm seriously troubled about God.

I think twice before giving Him a capital initial,
In fact I discover I've been resisting
Ever since schoolmasters behaved
Like gods, the idea of God as a Person.

The Trinity is three times as easy
(Protector, Friend and Inspiration)
But three's an exceedingly small crowd
And excludes a lot of non members;

And like most clubs, it's single sex.

Hiding under a leaf in Norfolk
I am quaking I think a bit,
Shaking, sitting in a plain chair.

Factually, though, it's nearly teatime,
Nearly sunset in the Dereham Road.
I'm sitting in the car outside St. Barnabas
Vicarage, writing in this notebook.

XLVI

the windows do not see the roofs
and dare not stare into this place
like prison bars denying each
side to the other they outface
crime punishment and boredom too

in uniforms of skin we put
each other to the question there
and strut our rank and flaunt our stance
with epaulettes of armpit hair
and brown or gold embellishments

alternate anger and relenting
soothing and shouting crying for
mercy where no mercy is
the room has walls but has no door
and there is no escape from us

so execute me execute
but don't stop torturing me too
this is us weightless upside down
it may be me it may be you
so long as neither one survives

stroking is honing for the cut
as clasp impales itself on kiss
and where I lick you scald and cry
electrodes in your fingers twitch
me into murdering all your calm

I do not know how we survive
I look at you who shared this death
who came this painfullest of journeys
gave your last gasp in the same breath
under a cracked and whitewashed ceiling

XLVII   Clacton

(Slap) Don't you – (slap) – don't you – don't you dare!
The promenade has low-railed grass beside it
And slopes, dusty, round flowerbeds towards the Pier.

Somebody's little boy's eternity is stinging and miserable.
He will never stop crying in my poem.

For our part, we are rediscovering dodgems,
And wear the stupid smile of the crisp-fed tripper
Who thinks he is getting his money's worth
And has forgotten economics;
And I forget and she why should she think for a moment
About the way economics has forgotten us?
I don't, as click clink the turnstile registers our arrival;
This cheap money is almost a pleasure to get rid of.

And whatever collisions screams surprises
Wheels rolling rumbling on metal
Fluctuate beneath them like weather in the basement,
Cicadas with blue fires in the wings of their heels
Keep up their chirping in the grey mesh ceiling.
In our car there is only one control: GO.
Steering is optional and you can skid like a rollerskate.

I hope he is smiling now but I don't feel very hopeful.

The Finger
Points
at the Moon

(SELECTIONS)

TO GASTON BERLEMONT

Inscriptions from Paris, May 1968.
The main sources are the walls of the
Sorbonne and of the streets in the
Latin Quarter. Some were written in
the Odéon Theatre.

Je suis venu
j'ai vu
j'ai cru

(Sorbonne)

*

Dessous les pavés c'est la plage ...

(Sorbonne)

*

Un homme n'est pas stupide ou intelligent:
il est libre ou il n'est pas.

(Medecine)

*

Etre libre en 1968, c'est participer.

(Sciences Po.)

*

La barricade ferme la rue mais ouvre la voie.

(Censier)

Défense de ne pas afficher.

(Sciences Po.)

*

Interdit d'Interdire.

(Sorbonne)

*

I came
I saw
I believed

*

UNDER THE COBBLESTONES – THE BEACH

*

It is not true that a man is either stupid or
intelligent: he is either free or not free.

*

If you are free in 1968, you take part.

*

**A barricade blocks the street
but opens the way.**

*

**People who don't stick bills
will be prosecuted**

*

PROHIBITING
PROHIBITED!

*

Ouvrons les portes
des asiles
des prisons
et autres
Facultés.

(Amphi. Musique, Nanterre)

*

Je décrète l'état de bonheur permanent.

(Sciences Po.)

*

Quand le doigt montre la lune, l'IMBECILE regarde le doigt.
Proverbe Chinois.

(Conservatoire Musique)

*

Je t'aime!!! Oh! Dites-le avec des pavés!!!!!

(Nanterre)

*

Dieu, je vous soupçonne d'être un intellectual de gauche.

(Condorcet)

*

Exagérer, c'est commencer d'inventer.

(Censier)

*

**Let us open the gates
of the asylums
of the prisons
and of the other
faculties**

*

I hereby decree a permanent state of happiness

*

WHEN THE FINGER POINTS AT THE MOON,
THE **FOOL** LOOKS AT THE FINGER
Chinese proverb.

*

I love you!!! Oh! Say it with cobblestones!!!!

*

I suspect you, God, of being a left-wing intellectual.

*

To exaggerate is to begin to invent

*

Millionaires de tous les pays unissez-vous,
le vent tourne.

(Censier)

*

On n'a (pas le temps d'écrire (!!)

(Nanterre)

*

Les murs ont des oreilles. Vos oreilles ont des murs.

(Sciences Pg.)

*

Les larmes des Philistins sont le nectar des dieux.

(Sorbonne)

*

Vous finirez tous par crever du confort.

(Nanterre)

*

Voyez sur ces murs la repression sexuelle et le refus
de soi-même. (A bas l'obscurantisme.)

(Censier)

*

L'action ne dois pas être une réaction mais une création.

(Censier)

*

***Millionaires of all lands, unite:
the wind is changing.***

*

*WHAT WE WANT IS
(The time to write!!!!)*

*

WALLS HAVE EARS. BUT YOUR EARS HAVE WALLS.

*

***The tears of the Philistines
are nectar to the gods***

*

YOU'LL ALL END UP DYING OF COMFORT

*

*Look: on these walls: sexual repression
and refusal of the self. (Down with obscurantism!)*

*

ACTION SHOULD NOT BE REACTION BUT CREATION

*

La forêt précède l'homme, le désert le suit.

(Sorbonne)

*

Cours camarade, le vieux est derrière toi.

(Sorbonne)

*

Regarde ton travail, le néant
et la torture y participent.

(Sorbonne)

*

Nous sommes tous des 'indésirables'.

(Beaux-Arts)

*

Je ne sais pas qu'écrire mais j'aimerais en dire de belles
et je ne sais pas.

(Censier)

*

Déjà 10 jours de bonheur.

(Censier)

*

L'économie est blessée, qu'elle crève.

(Censier)

*

The forest confronts man:
the desert follows him.

*

Run, comrade! The old man is after you!

*

**Consider your work:
emptiness and torture
play a part in it.**

*

WE ARE ALL OF US
UNDESIRABLES

*

*I don't know what to write
but I'd like to write something terrific
but I don't know*

*

10 DAYS' HAPPINESS ALREADY

*

**The economy is reeling . . .
– let it drop dead.**

*

Soyez salés, pas sucrés!

(Odéon)

*

Qui parle de l'amour détruit l'amour.

(Nanterre)

*

Je suis marxiste tendance Groucho.

(Nanterre)

*

Soyez réalistes
demandez
l'impossible

(Censier)

*

Le vent se lève il faut tenter de vivre

(Nanterre)

*

Bourgeois, parvenus qui tirent l'echelle après eux
et ne veulent pas laisser monter le peuple.
Victor Hugo.

(Sorbonne)

*

BE SALT
NOT SWEET!

*

Whoever speaks of love destroys love

*

I am a Marxist
– with Groucho tendencies.

*

BE REALISTIC:
ASK FOR THE IMPOSSIBLE!

*

the wind is rising
we must try to live

*

The Middle Classes: jumped-up individuals
who pull the ladder up after them
and won't let the people climb.
                                    Victor Hugo.

*

Pas de replâtrage, la structure est pourrie.

(Fac. de Droit, Assas)

*

Etes-vous des <u>consommateurs</u> ou bien des <u>participants?</u>

(Odéon)

*

L'âge d'or était l'âge où l'or ne régnait pas.
Le veau d'or est toujours de boue.

(Odéon)

*

Embrasse ton amour sans lâcher ton fusil.

(Odéon)

*

Je me propose d'agiter et d'inquiéter les gens.
Je ne vends pas le pain mais la levure.
Unamuno.

(Odéon)

*

La Révolution doit cesser d'être pour EXISTER.

(Nanterre)

*

No plasterers wanted:
the structure is unsound.

*

ARE YOU CONSUMING, OR PARTICIPATING?

*

The Golden Age
was precisely the age
in which gold did *not* reign.
A golden calf is always made of mud.

*

Put your arm round your lover
but don't let go of your gun

*

I want to agitate, to disturb other people:
I am not selling bread, but yeast.
Unamuno.

*

THE REVOLUTION MUST CEASE TO **BE**
IN ORDER TO **EXIST**

*

Jeunes femmes rouges toujours plus belles.

(Fac. de Medecine)

*

L'imagination prend le pouvoir.

(Sciences Po.)

*

Violez votre ALMA MATER.

(Nanterre)

*

Parlez à vos voisins.

(Censier)

*

La poésie est dans la rue.

(Odéon)

Young women who are Red are always more beautiful

*

THE IMAGINATION IS SEIZING POWER

*

violate your Alma Mater

*

SPEAK TO YOUR NEIGHBOURS

*

Poetry
is
in
the
street

Moons
and Tides,
Walberswick

FOR VIC AND LENNIE

1

New moon high water now and calm
But not unruffled by a bright
Breeze at elevenses I jumped
Out of bed as late last night
Was shattered with the barrier

Let us stay on our separate sides
Old leather man you see the sea
Roll out the map of Europe bang
Or what the hell I made some tea
And went to look out at the window

Some but no fatal letters some
But not outrageously good looking
Visitors with fishing rods
And the bread came and smells of cooking
Rose and silence in the village

2

New moon and darker by blown clouds
Across the sky from north to south
Across the stars as brown as smoke
But in the river's dripping mouth
What herring fish for in the dark

Fertile and phosphorescent swell
The boat goes over rocked afloat
Oars mixing milk beneath the glass
Surfaces where quiet float
Millions more than shine below

And grounding on the farther bank
Rubs on hard sand the bow wave spreads
Green lights along high water mark
Feel for the post tie up boots tread
Slow home but stars spring out each step

3

Spring or summer came the third
Of May after the woods the beach
Glared the North Sea roared and would
Not let go growled over each
Pebble there was coal washed up

Three miles I picked coal and four
Places hid it and went back
Next afternoon the wind again
But clear and in pale sand the black
Diamonds rubbed smooth by pebbles

Heavy too I was surprised
Lifting the sack tied with an old
Piece of net then saw the moon
First time white on blue the gold
Afternoon stopped at the clouds

4

Half moon half moon the second half
The half of darkness as the first
Heavy yellow set behind
The sea wall over meadows cursed
Four years ago with floods of salt

Neaps but the wind kept up and kept
High tides high and hardly let
Ebb tides out but covered with
Hissing white and I forget
If I ever saw such fury

Sunday at noon a black ketch rode
Steadier in that cable stiff
Roaring than the night before
Dragged the red buoy but held and if
Too huge had not been there before

5

High tide is simple harbour full
At low tide in a shallow cup
Evil fortunes are revealed
Bladder wracked gap toothed stick up
Stumps of piles
                that was dry land

Scoured and now the ferry hut
And Bob's shed are the last that stand
The weathervane has rusted stiff
The clay causeway has caries and
The rats come out and graze like sheep

Come zenith of the rounding moon
Cover the weeping river mud
Green pebbles rubble wrack and slime
All the fireworks here are dud
Bring us high water and high time

6

Slack water now the boats go round
As anticlockwise round the lows
Wind southwest and force 3 to 4
Mingles with sea breeze the sun blows
The hanging weeds left at low tide

Moon rises over German Bight
Korean fishermen out early
Wait for dawn old Bob comes tired
Across the shingle with his curly
Dogs that look as old as he

The moon will be more round the boats
Are facing down the rising tide
Cumulus clouds build up inland
Even last year's death has died
Swallows and terns have come again

7

Moon clearer than blueprint can print
A rounder shape than yesterday
Afternoon sharp on the arc
With tangent light shaded the way
Delicacy can be exact

Between in time this negative
Daylight moon and moonlight which
Dinks and I rowed under from
The Harbour Inn side feeling rich
With experience and joy

There was a broad wing stretched across
The clear northwest its trailing edge
Glimmering in blue dusk was high
Water low cloud drove a wedge
Of mauve between it and the sky

8

Cloud lavender two rooks fly home
Close to the wrinkled water climb
At shingle over sea wall black
All else is grey this is the time
Before the time before the last

The clipped coin of the rising moon
Shows primrose yellow through a gap
More black than white an oystercatcher
Cries as mournful down the map
Of marshes it propels a beak

Up the harbour a grey swell
Heaves and scours the beach above
The concrete wall and wets the slip
Where two people perhaps in love
Learning to look at water stare

9

From sinking sulphur yellow moon
Behind the dead black village to
Dawn breaking over lighthouse wink
Red under rose and paling blue
The long beach like a torrent roared

The moon blackened the silhouettes
Of trees new leaves were filling in
And dimmed the orange vigil of
The phone box on the village green
But yellow she looked sick to death

If coming back the sinking glare
Of going out before became
A following and rising till
At the back door it was the same
Still dawn was younger than us all

10

At long last came up gold and round
The almost perfect moon and stood
Over the still shifting heaving
Grey North Sea while from the wood
Blew the scent of meadow grass

Under the long going light
Came quicksilver flood tide over
Wall and slipway the first star
Was a four mooned planet drove a
Solitary course to set

Two vapour trails twisted like salt
Poured down that high blue the moon
Brightened in the seadusk over
Gold horizon line and soon
Gold to where the waves broke spilled

Perfect as the earth came up
Darkening before it struck
Out a corner of the light
Waterfowl began to cluck
Sleeptalk dream talk and foreboding

Within the hour the moon was blood
The comet showed northwest but faint
Monday the thirteenth of the month
Wanted as powerful a saint
As any in the calendar

Blood on the month dark on the bright
Virgin and a Druid curse
Horror struck through telescope
There was no blood it was worse
Swollen dark and putrefied

Plaguestruck all the stars began
To shine aloud a nightingale
Tuned to sing but the wind blew
Clouds across began to wail
Soft and sudden in the eaves

Down the flood tide sailed a trawler
Slow into the moon a white
Masthead light and starboard green
Out into uncertain night
Only Ronaldsway had calm

Here was victory and a grave
But where's a girl to play the flute
That was full moon as full can be
O passion for the absolute
Newest of all puts out the sun

Quia Amore
Langueo

Dedicated to

Sisters Alies, Elizabeth, Sarah, Deborah, Ann-Marie, Maria Joseph, Mary Garnet, Lai See, Paula, Judith, Gillian, Gill Price, Deirdre, Deirdre Mary, Shelagh, Anita, Liza, Patricia, Teresa, Wendy, Rachel, Stella, Mildred, Joyce, Kay, Penny, Maria, Anna, Irene, Mary Louisa, Lynn-Marie, Sara, Bertranda, Mary Edward, Dot and Fee.

I

THE APPEAL OF
THE BLESSED VIRGIN MARY
TO MAN

In an alcove of a tower,
As I stood musing on the moon,
A crowned queen of great honour
I saw in a spiritual vision;
And she lamented there alone,
For human souls were wrapped in woe,
'I cannot leave mankind alone,
Quia amore langueo.

I long for love of man my brother,
I plead for pardon of his vice,
I am his mother – I can no other –
Why should I my dear child despise?
Though he provoke me in diverse wise
And through his frailty fall, even so
We must pity him until he rise,
Quia amore langueo.

I bide, I bide in great longing,
I watch till men my love will crave;
I complain for pity of their pining;
Should they beg mercy, they would it have,
Sue to me, soul, and I shall save;
Bid me, my child, and I shall go;
You prayed me never but my Son forgave,
Quia amore langueo.

I am mankind's help, acknowledging;
When they will call, I shall restore;
I love to save my own offspring.
Now will I tell of this matter more:
No wonder my heart to Jesu cling;
I am his mother, what else can I do?
For his sake have I this worshipping,
Quia amore langueo.

Why was I crowned and made a queen?
Why was I called of mercy the well?
Why should an earthly woman have been
Placed high in heaven, above angel?
For thee, mankind; it is truth I tell;
Ask me for help and I shall do
What I was ordained for: keep thee from hell,
Quia amore langueo.

Now, man, have mind on me for ever;
Look on thy love thus languishing!
Let us never from each other dissever;
My help is thine own; creep under my wing.
Thy sister's a queen, thy brother a king,
Inheritance sure! Son, come thereunto:
Join hands with me, and learn thou to sing:
"Quia amore langueo."

II

THE APPEAL OF
CHRIST
TO MANKIND

In a valley of this restless mind
I sought in mountain and in mead,
Trusting a true love for to find.
Upon an hill then took I heed;
A voice I heard (and near I yede)
In great dolour complaining tho:
'See, dear soul, how my sides bleed,
Quia amore langueo.'

Upon this hill I found a tree;
Under the tree a man sitting;
From head to foot wounded was he;
His heart's blood I saw bleeding.
A seemly man to be a king,
A gracious face to look unto:
I asked him why he had paining.
Quia amore langueo.

I am true love that false was never.
My sister, man's soul, I loved her thus;
Because I would in no wise dissever
I left my kingdom glorious;
I purveyed her a palace full precious,
She fled, I followed, I loved her so
That I suffered this pain piteous,
Quia amore langueo.

yede went
tho then

My fair love, and my spouse bright!
I saved her from beating and she hath me bet;
I clothed her in grace and heavenly light:
This bloody shirt she hath on me set.
For love-longing yet would I not let
(Sweet strokes are these, lo!)
I have loved her ever as I her het,
                    Quia amore langueo.

I crowned her with bliss, and she me with thorn;
I led her to chamber, and she me to die;
I brought her to worship, and she me to scorn;
I did her reverence, and she me villainy.
To love one who loves is no mastery;
Her hate made never my love her foe.
Ask me then no question why:
                    Quia amore langueo.

Look unto mine hands, man!
These gloves were given me when I her sought.
They be not white, but red and wan;
Embroidered with blood my spouse them brought.
They will not off, I loose them not,
I woo her with them wherever she go.
These hands for her so friendly fought
                    Quia amore langueo

bet   beaten
let   stop
het   promised
wan   (in a now obsolete sense) of an unwholesome
colour, livid, leaded-hued

Marvel not, man, though I sit still:
See, love hath shod me wonder strait,
Buckled my feet (as was her will)
With a sharp nail: well mayest thou wait!
In my love was never deceit:
All my members I have opened her-to;
My body I made her heart's bait,
           Quia amore langueo.

In my side I have made her nest;
Look in! How wet a wound is here!
This is her chamber, here shall she rest
That she and I may sleep in-fere,
Here may she wash, if any filth were;
Here is seat for all her woe:
Come when she will, she shall have cheer,
           Quia amore langueo.

I will abide till she be ready,
I will her sue if she say nay,
If she be reckless, I will be greedy,
If she be dangerous, I will her pray.
If she weep, then bide I ne may;
My arms are spread to clip her me-to.
Cry once, I come. Now, soul, assay,
           Quia amore langueo.

bait   resting place (on a journey)
in-fere   together (originally) on a journey
dangerous   difficult to deal with, not affable (ME)

I sit on this hill for to see far,
I look into the valley my spouse to see:
Now runs she away-ward, now comes she near,
But out of my sight she may not flee.
Some lie in wait, to make their prey flee:
I run ahead, to chastise her foe.
Return again, my spouse, unto me,
                    Quia amore langueo.

Fair love, let us go play.
Apples are ripe in my garden.
I shall thee clothe in a new array;
Thy meat shall be milk, honey and wine,
Fair love, let us go dine:
Thy sustenance is in my scrip, lo!
Tarry thou not, fair spouse of mine,
                    Quia amore langueo.

If thou be foul I shall make thee clean;
If thou be sick, I shall thee heal;
If thou mourn aught, I shall with thee moan:
Why wilt thou not, fair love, with me deal?
Foundest thou ever love so leal?
What wouldst thou, soul, that I should do?
I may not unkindly to thee appeal,
                    Quia amore langueo.

What shall I do with my fair spouse
But wait for her in all gentleness,
Till that she look out of her house
Of fleshly affection? Love mine she is.
Her bed is made, her bolster is bliss,
Her chamber is chosen, there is no more.
Look out at me through the window of kindness,
                Quia amore langueo.

My love is in her chamber; hold your peace!
Make ye no noise, but let her sleep.
My babe I would not were in dis-ease;
I cannot hear my dear child weep.
With my pap I shall her keep:
Marvel not though I tend to her so:
This wound in my side had ne'er been so deep
          But *Quia amore langueo.*

Long thou for a love never so high,
My love is more than thine may be.
Thou weepest, thou gladdest, I sit thee by;
Yet would thou once, love, look unto me!
But should I always nourish thee
With children's meat? – Nay, love, not so:
I will prove thy love with adversity,
                Quia amore langueo.

Wax not weary, my own wife!
What meed is it always to live in comfort?
In tribulation I reign more rife,
Oftentimes, than in disport.
In weal and in woe I am aye to support:
Mine own wife, go not me fro!
Thy meed is marked when thou art mort,
                    Quia amore langueo.

meed reward

Five Peace Poems

FOR MICHAEL HAMBURGER

Peace Poem

waking at five or so to white
sky and various bird beginnings
from exhausting dreams of past
emotional encounters I can
rest at last in a small room

lying still considering
whether to go back to sleep
seeing the sky go colours of
sunrise I begin to wonder
how the tree looks and the wall

downstairs in the shadow of
the houses sleepers lie asleep
in Kenninghall in Diss in Mellis
bliss behind the children's eyelids
all alone in morning silence

what is peace if it is not
loving indiscriminately
others? Watching over all
human sleep and knowing there's
no need and every need to do so?

what is peace but watching while
being loved and cared for by
the very clouds and trees and grass
nourishing earth and candid sky
breakneck rivers rising tides?

newspapers at seven o'clock
are laying on the day the grey
word of war and world of worry
all I want's a weather forecast
promising there'll be more weather

Lesson

Elementary peace, or prep-school peace if you like,
Means that when the boy you are sitting on says I give in,
Or if you prefer him to do it in Latin, PAX,
You stop twisting his arm or strangling him
Or doing perhaps even more unpleasant things
Which of course have to be done, it's a point of honour,
And get off his weedy carcase and let him go
And blub to his mum or grass on you or pretend
He didn't deserve what he got: so long as he knows
That you are the master and he has no cause to rejoice.

Advanced peace, or Peace in the Real World,
Is the same. The thing you have to bear in mind
Is this: at the End of the Day it's Up to You
To Make it Stick. Negotiate if you like,
– That is, if you can afford to, – but From Strength.
Remember, peace is not some disgusting form
Of intercourse with all and sundry. Peace
Is a matter of Strong Government. Leadership.
And Peace With Honour Is Worth Fighting For.

A Visit to London

CHARGE SHEET. On Wednesday 22nd. February 1984
at Bridge Street S.W.1. you did without lawful authority
or excuse wilfully obstruct the free passage along the
highway. *Con Sec 137(1) Highways Act 1980*

On Wednesday 22 Feb 1984 wilfully obstructing Steven West
a Constable of the Metropolitan Police force in the
execution of his duty. *Con.Sec 51(3) Police Act 1964*

The theology for this afternoon
Is, as usual, love.
Not abstract love to faceless multitudes,
But love that is always there to do, like work;
And can't be done enough of, can't be finished.
And much as I'm loved,
(And I must be, look at the pavement under my feet,
Look at the railings standing reliable,
The sky lighting my life),
I can't give enough for others; I can only
Give what I can. At least I can today.

This afternoon at two o'clock love locks
Thirteen of us to the House of Commons railings,
Unfolding banners posters pieces of paper
Saying the arms race is a violation
Of international law and of conventions
Agreed by various governments including
Our own. And I am here with the other twelve
Because my government is breaking
Higher laws than these.
I mean Christ's laws for the workers of the world
And for those who imagine they're working it.

All I lost was my chains and one of the padlocks:
The police kept them, I didn't have time to claim them.

Big Ben towers over us silent under repair.
The police have walkie talkies
And in about seven minutes
Vans and bolt cutters.
One minute we are smiling and talking to strangers
Who don't seem the least bit strange,
And the next the party's over.

Round various corners there is Cannon Row:
A charge room where we are charged
And small Victorian cells.
Holmes takes the wooden bed,
Watson the mattress on the floor
And Oscar Wilde a couple of pillows and a blanket.

February daylight wanes
In the cast iron window panes.

Later we get fingerprinted.
Later still tea from the canteen.
Police wait on prisoners
Like Christmas Day in the barracks.

The food is not bad but the music is atrocious:
All night long the drunken marine engineer
Curses and sings.
All night long they come round shouting:
Are you all right?
Are we all right? We are all right all night.

Morning comes with strong stale smells of poverty
And comings and goings in the corridor,
Cell doors banging but the feet are quiet.

It's almost never our cell door they open.
The big blue bus with its bogsized compartments
Takes us sightseeing. We are one of the sights.
The Horse Guards Trafalgar Square The National Gallery
And into the back yard of Bow Street Magistrates' Court.

Another cell. One thief, one A.B.H.
In a very smart suit;
Two peaceniks fresh from the nick in Cannon row.
Slightly selfconscious smiles and conscious silence.
A neat young woman gaoler
Brings us water in plastic cups:
It's nice and cold.

The Magistrate looks up, witty, fresh, clean shaven:
He won't accept we obstructed
Both the highway and the police.
Just the highway.
Have I got anything to say?
I say it as fast as I can for fear of being cut short.
"Yes. I accept it's a matter of conscience."
"Thank you, Sir." (What is this Thank you sir?)
Conditional discharge.
Sounds like a government transmitted disease.

But I'm off.
Four of us are off.
The others are pleading Not Guilty.
My excuse is, I'm suppose to be reading my verses
This evening at the Poetry Society.
It's embarrassing. They're paying me fifty pounds.
There's drinks with the Polish delegation. And expenses.
But I'm not going to charge them for my bed and breakfast.

Mountains

Oh the terrific male thrill of conquest!
The utter wonderfulness of surmounting
obstacles, driving hard bargains
with porters, establishing base camps,
winning upwards, always Excelsior,
(I may be some time
over this bit of celebration),
breathing increasingly heady,
decreasingly lungworthy air,
surveying that of which
the intrepid mountaineer
may justly be called monarch;
to plant, finally,
the symbol beloved of airlines,
fairgrounds and protonazis:
the Union (No surrender!)
Jack (I'm all right)
on the uttermost pinnacle
of the highest available mountain
because it is there!

Meanwhile, "deep in the province
of Fukien, where few Europeans
have ever penetrated" from whence
comes Jackson's Ching Wo tea,
"which is best drunk with a slice of lemon"
(I quote from the 8 oz.
226 gm. tin)

there are two old Chinese persons
sitting on a verandah
under a bamboo leaf roof
sipping perhaps Ching Wo

anyway tea
and turning from time to time
to look at the lilac
indigo
purple
far-off
mountains
(because they are there)

Office Work

plane trees and pavements
passively witness
nice chaps arriving
nice girls departing
on the steps of
the Ministry of
let us politely
call it Defence

fully employed and
highly respectable
they carry out the
unexciting
but essential
duties assigned them

they are not excitable
overemotional
or suspicious
only anxious
to perform correctly
tasks or at least to
convey that impression

decent suits and
sensible skirts
wear very gradually
and promotion
gradually comes
possibly somewhat
tardily and more
often to others
than oneself

similar sunlit
scenes were repeated
in Berlin Vienna
Prague Stettin
Warsaw Brussels
Budapest
from 1933
to 1944
(the thousand-year Reich)

corridors offices
filing cabinets
strong manila envelopes

classification
concentration
evacuation
deportation
finally resolved
themselves into holocaust
regrettable necessity
for the establishment
of a new improved
order of society

nuclear physics
secret research
spectacular testing
and experiment
in never never deserts
and in the Japanese
history lab.
cold war deterrence
overkill
first strike capability
all eventually

signify holocaust
regrettable necessity
(in the event)
for the defence of
the free society
free of liberal
leftist atheist
liberationist
Marxist terrorist
totalitarian
forces of evil
enemies of freedom
and democracy

(market forces
dog eat hot dog
peasant eat agent orange)

hell on earth
began in the ghettoes and
finally reached
the Führer's bunker

16 years later
in Jerusalem
the other Adolf
Eichmann a boring
ministry employee
remembered best
the irritating slowness
of promotion
and how he'd never
hated the Jews

New and Recent Poetry from Anvil

Nina Bogin
The Winter Orchards

Nina Cassian
Take My Word for It

Martina Evans
All Alcoholics Are Charmers

Michael Hamburger
Intersections

James Harpur
Oracle Bones

Anthony Howell
Selected Poems

Marius Kociejowski
Music's Bride

Peter Levi
Viriditas

Gabriel Levin
Ostraca

Thomas McCarthy
Mr Dineen's Careful Parade

Stanley Moss
Asleep in the Garden

Dennis O'Driscoll
Weather Permitting

Peter Scupham
Night Watch

Daniel Weissbort
What Was All the Fuss About?